A Gift For:

_____

From:

_____

Copyright © 2018 Hallmark Licensing, LLC

Published by Hallmark Gift Books,
a division of Hallmark Cards, Inc.,
Kansas City, MO 64141
Visit us on the Web at Hallmark.com.

All rights reserved. No part of this publication may be reproduced, transmitted, or stored in any form or by any means without the prior written permission of the publisher.

Editorial Director: Delia Berrigan
Art Director: Chris Opheim
Designer: Brian Pilachowski
Production Designer: Dan Horton

ISBN: 978-1-63059-695-8
1XKT2340

Made in China
0718

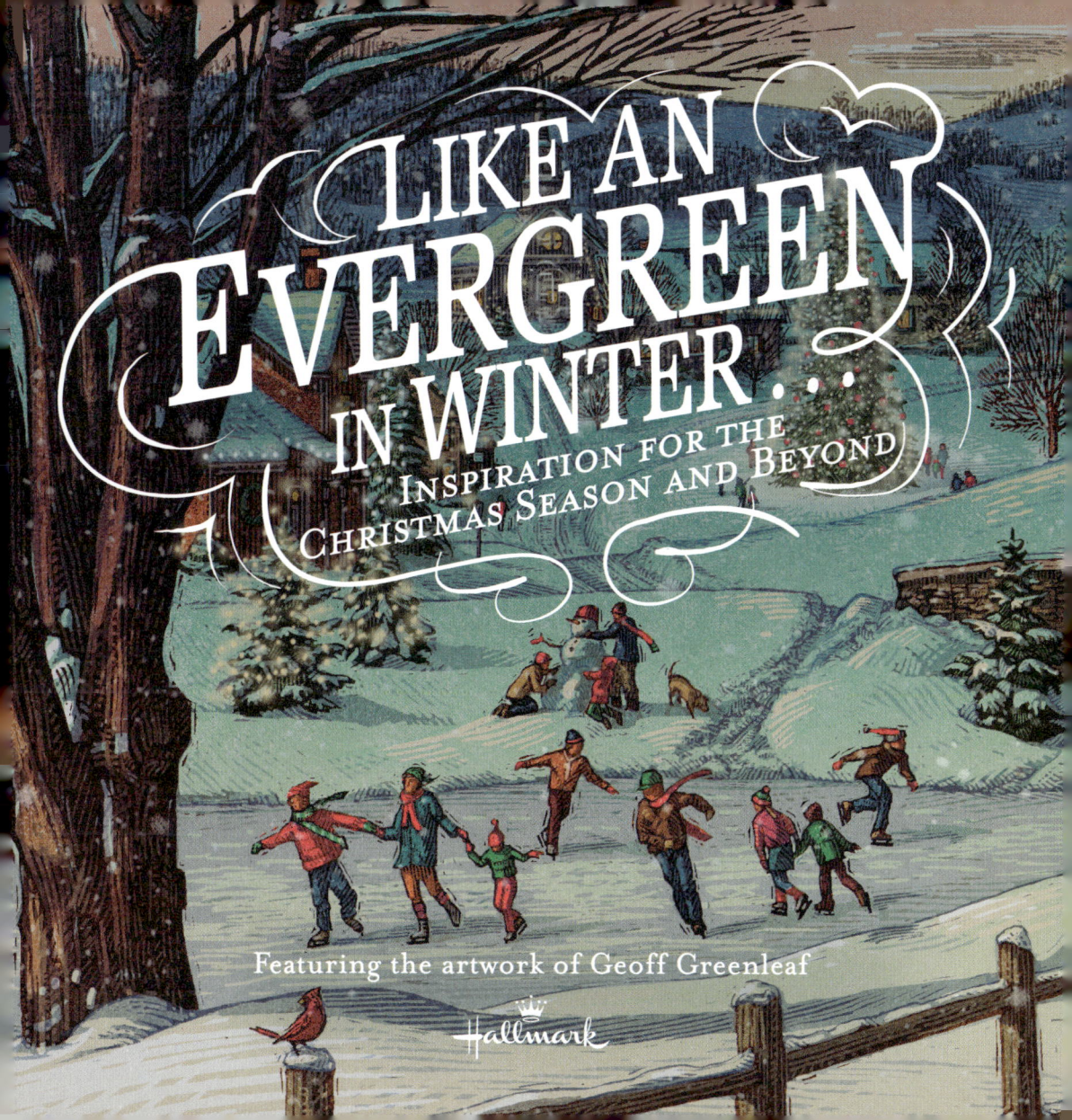

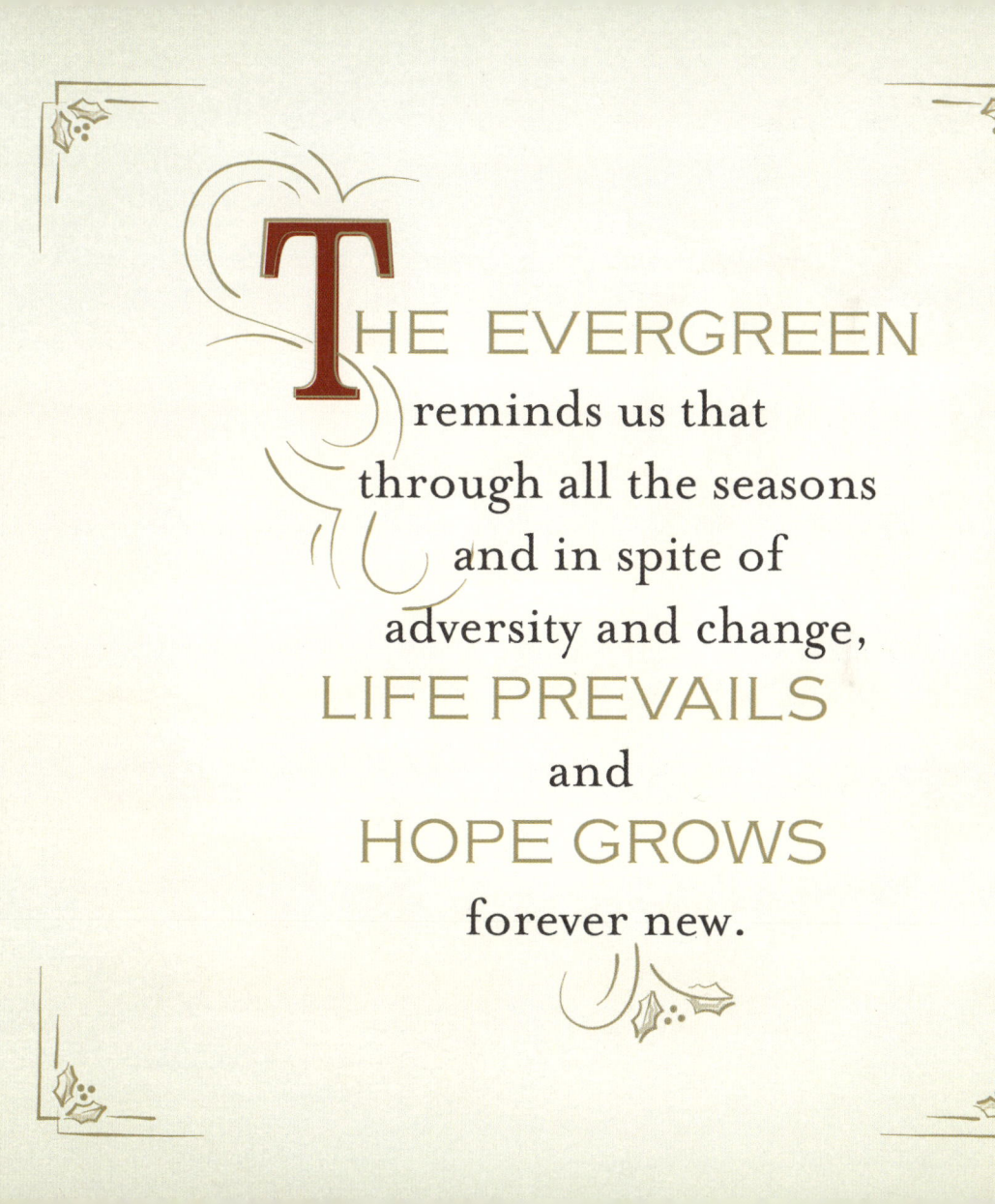

The evergreen
reminds us that
through all the seasons
and in spite of
adversity and change,
LIFE PREVAILS
and
HOPE GROWS
forever new.

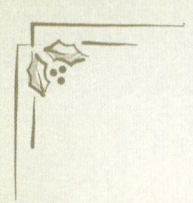
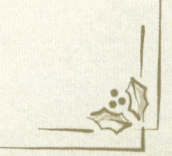

CHRISTMAS
is a golden time,
lovingly guarded in
OUR HEARTS,
that we rediscover
year after year.

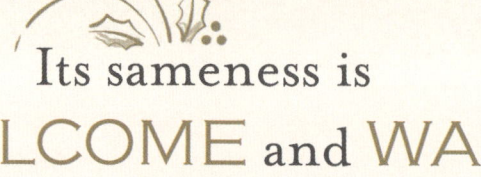

Its sameness is
WELCOME and WARM,
COMFORTING and GENTLE—

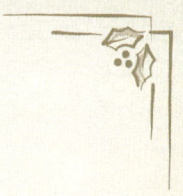

a REFUGE in a world
of dizzying CHANGE
and COMPETITION.

Home is very much
a part of the
GLOW, the WARMTH,
the precious HAVEN
that is Christmas.

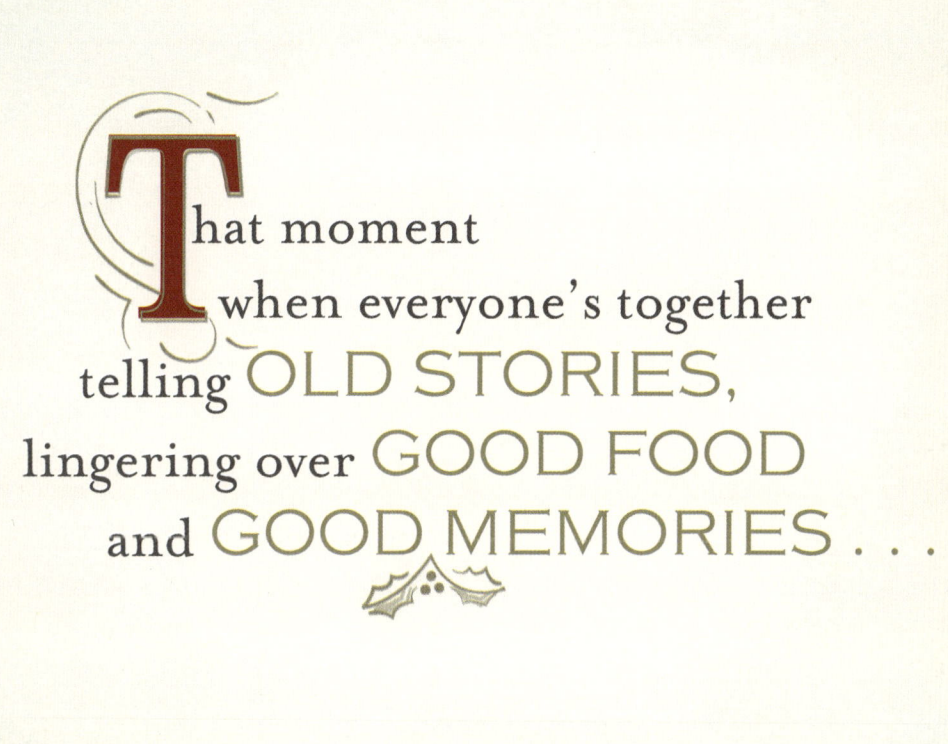

That moment when everyone's together telling OLD STORIES, lingering over GOOD FOOD and GOOD MEMORIES . . .

. . . when you have the thought
that right here in this room
is EVERYTHING
THAT MATTERS most . . .

. . . that's when you know
IT'S CHRISTMAS.

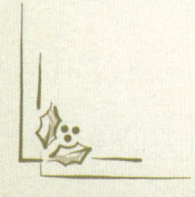

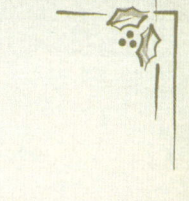

Close your eyes
and listen,
and you MAY HEAR IT . . .

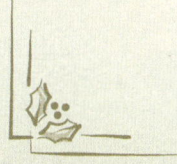

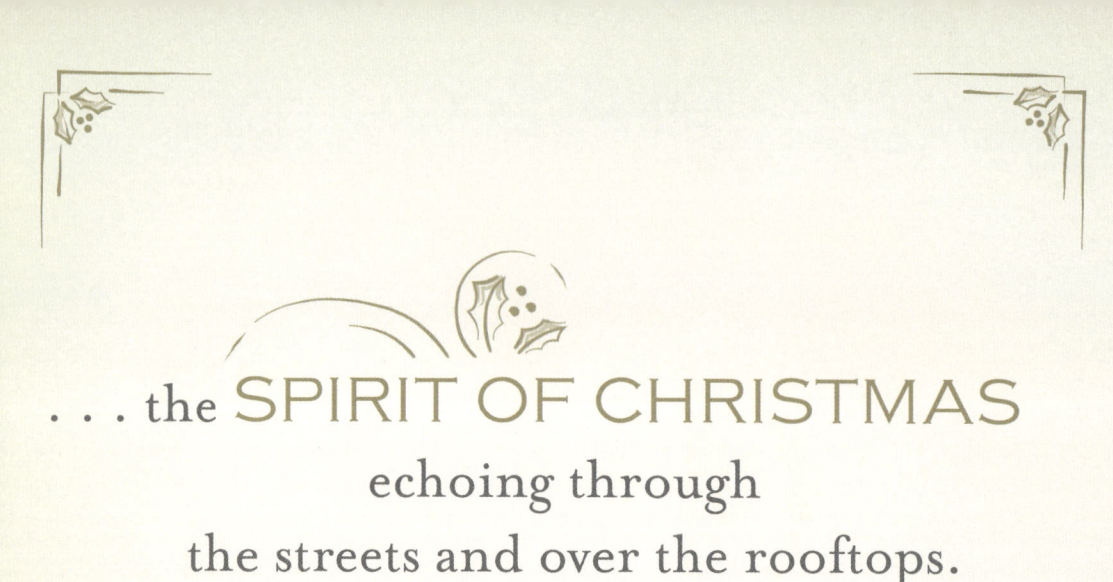

. . . the SPIRIT OF CHRISTMAS
echoing through
the streets and over the rooftops.

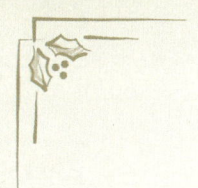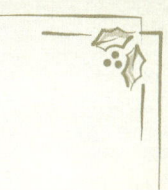

Sometimes it sounds
like the LAUGHTER
of CHILDREN.

Sometimes it sounds
like a CAROL
or a GIFT being shaken.

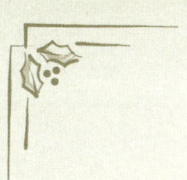

And sometimes,
for those whose
HEARTS are filled
with the WONDER
of CHRISTMAS,
it rings out like a bell
from SANTA'S
own magical sleigh.

Christmas means a warm, full, messy HOME . . .

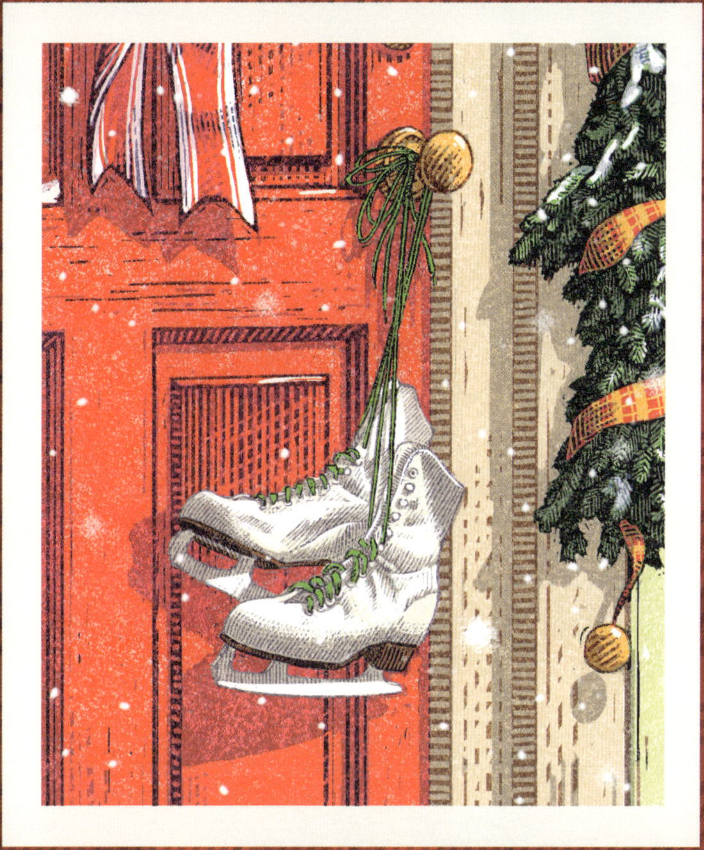

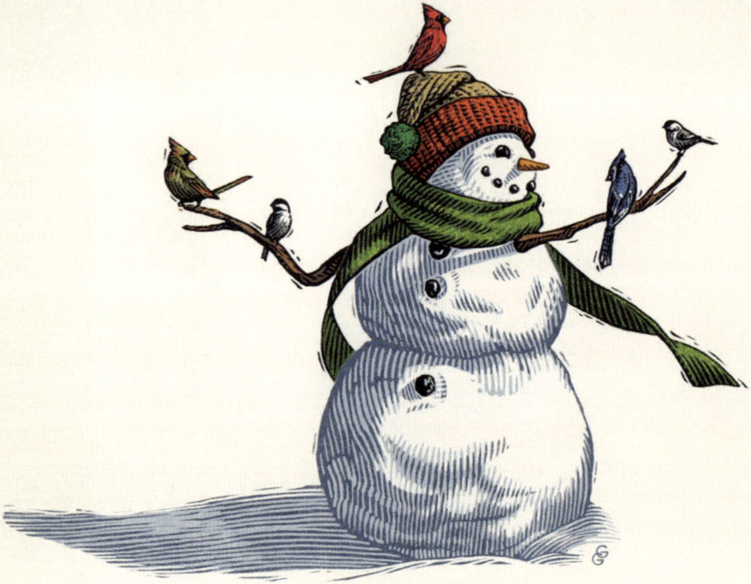

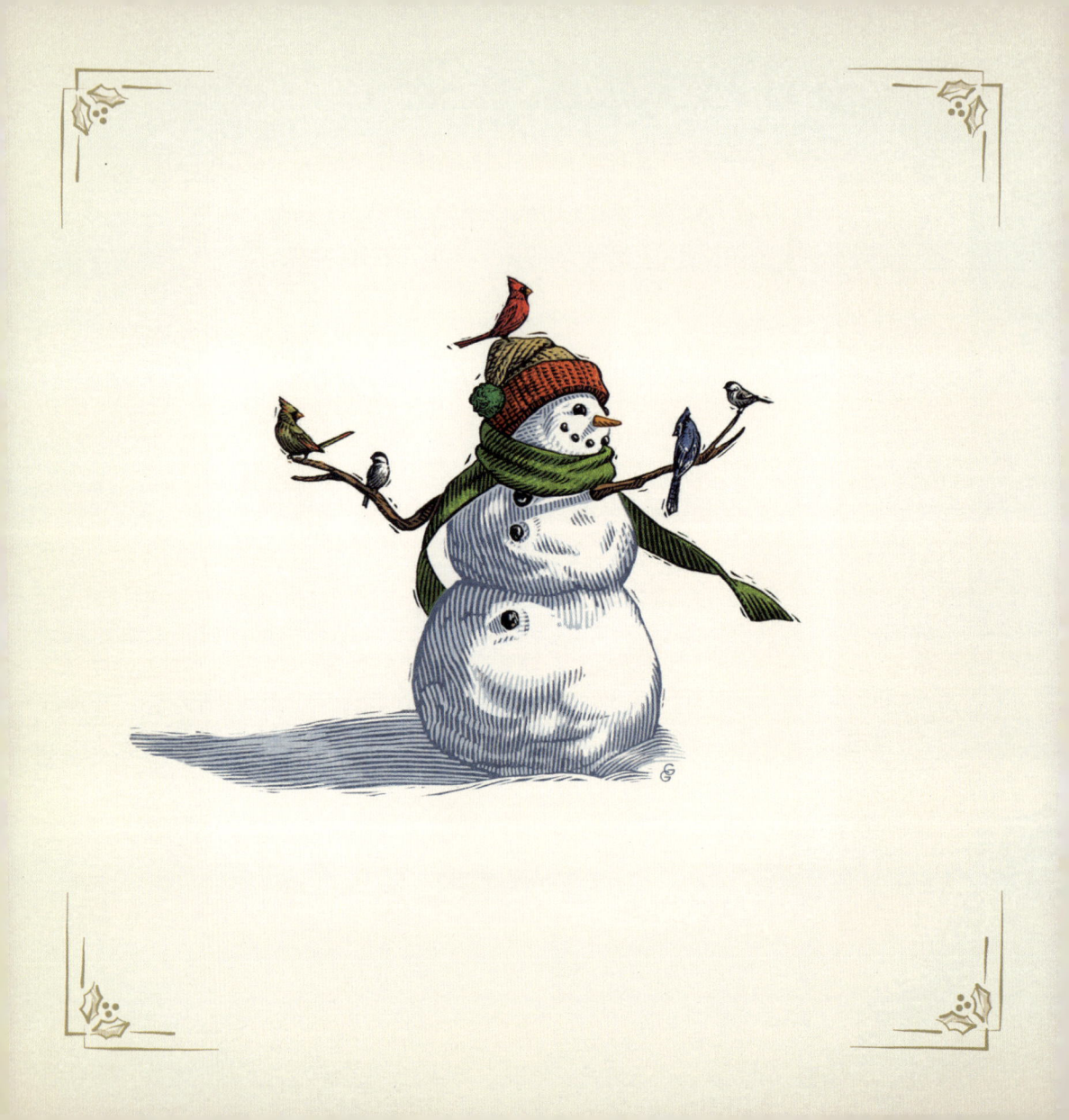

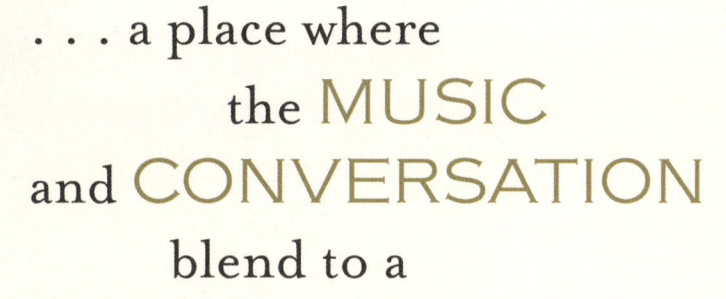

. . . a place where
the MUSIC
and CONVERSATION
blend to a
RHYTHM all their own.

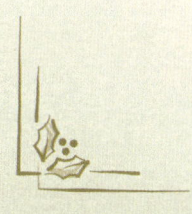

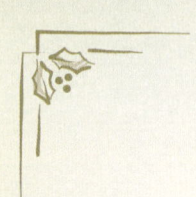

It means people passing from room to room and a front DOOR that NEVER stays CLOSED for long.

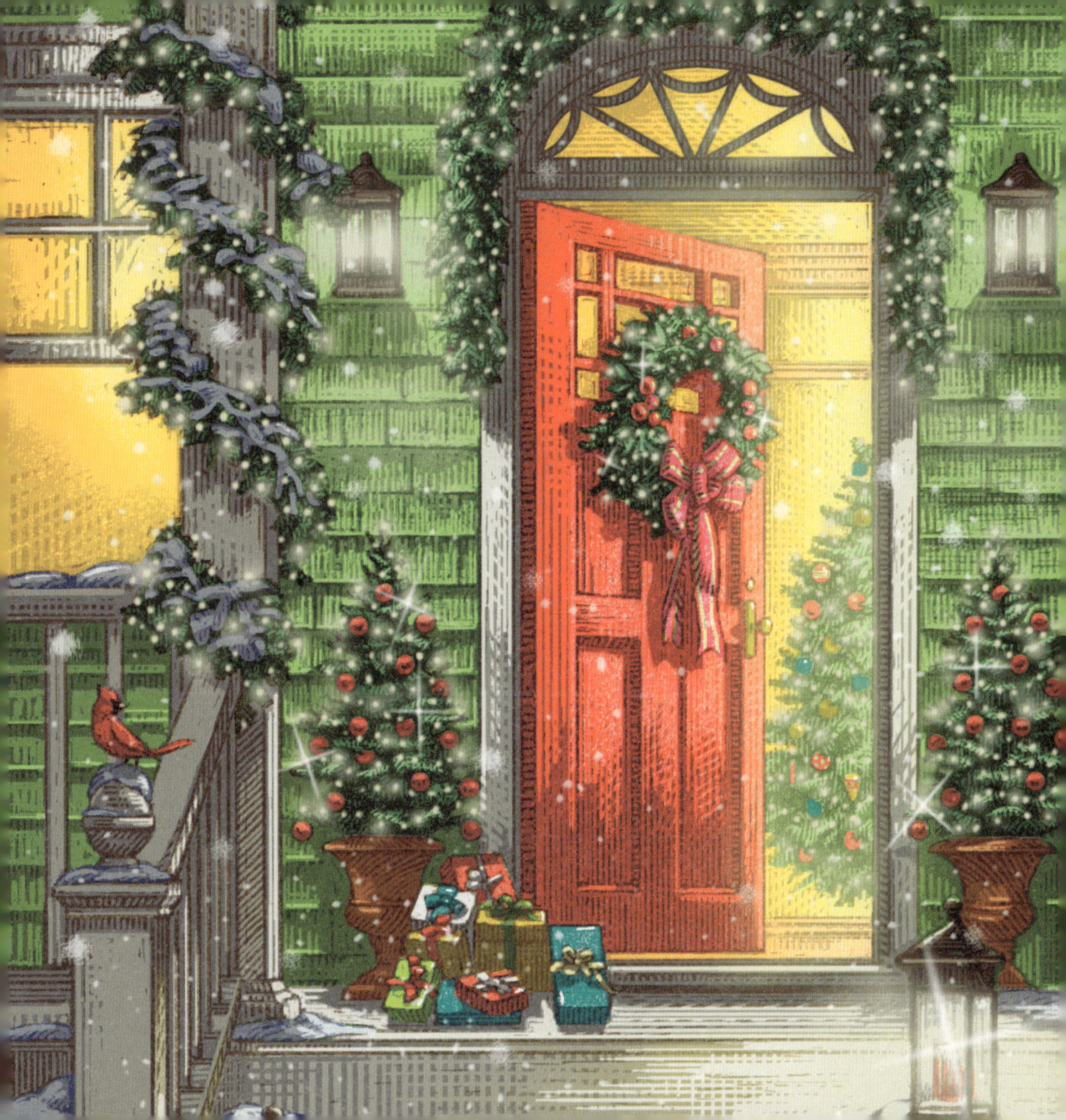

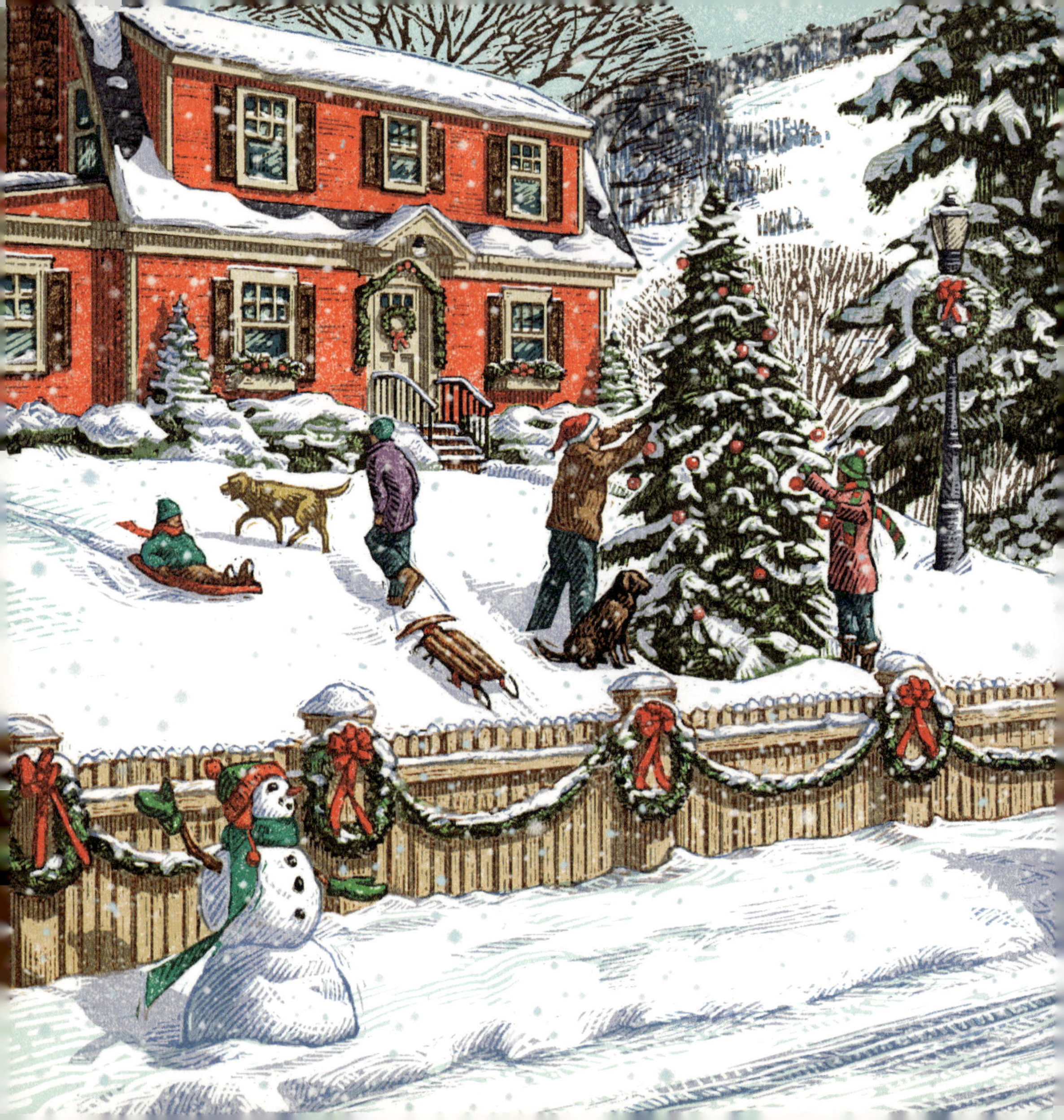

Christmas means
nothing's in its place
and EVERYONE
YOU LOVE
is right where
they should be . . .

. . . TOGETHER.

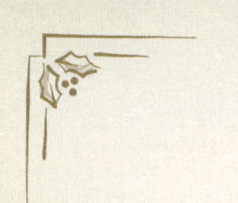

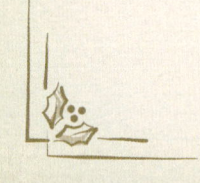

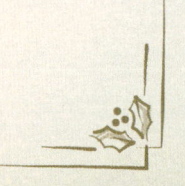

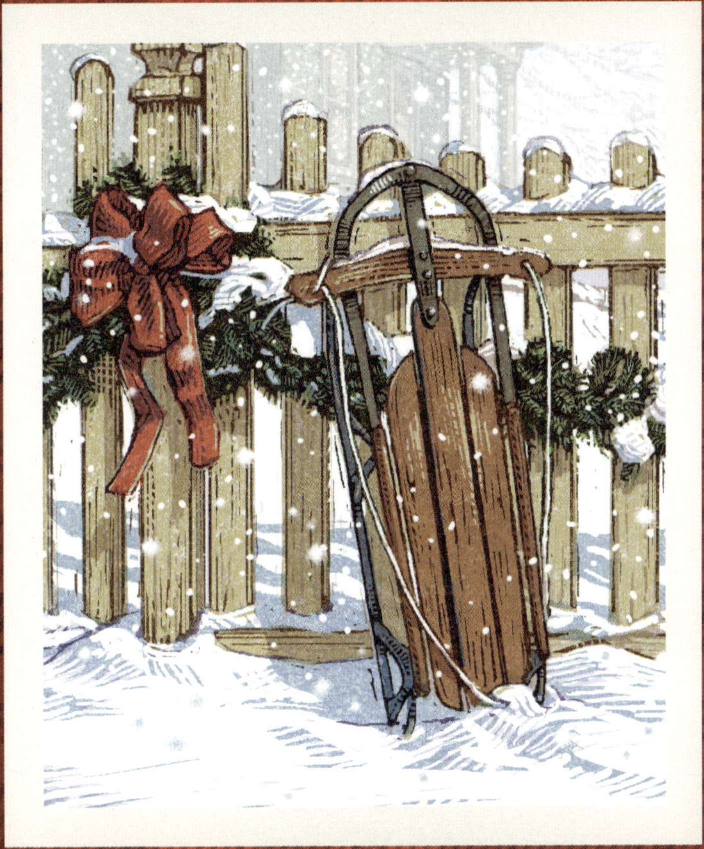

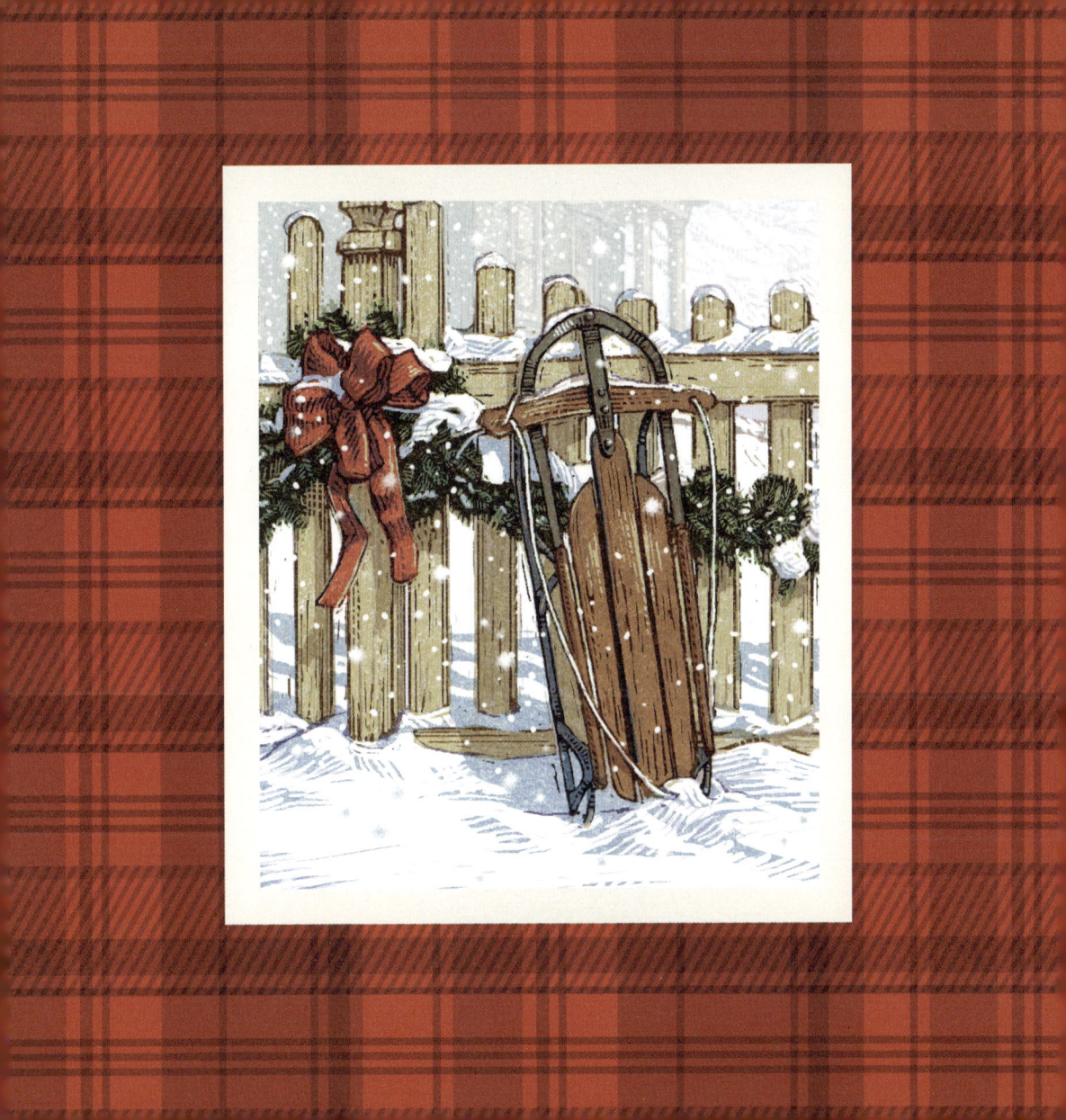

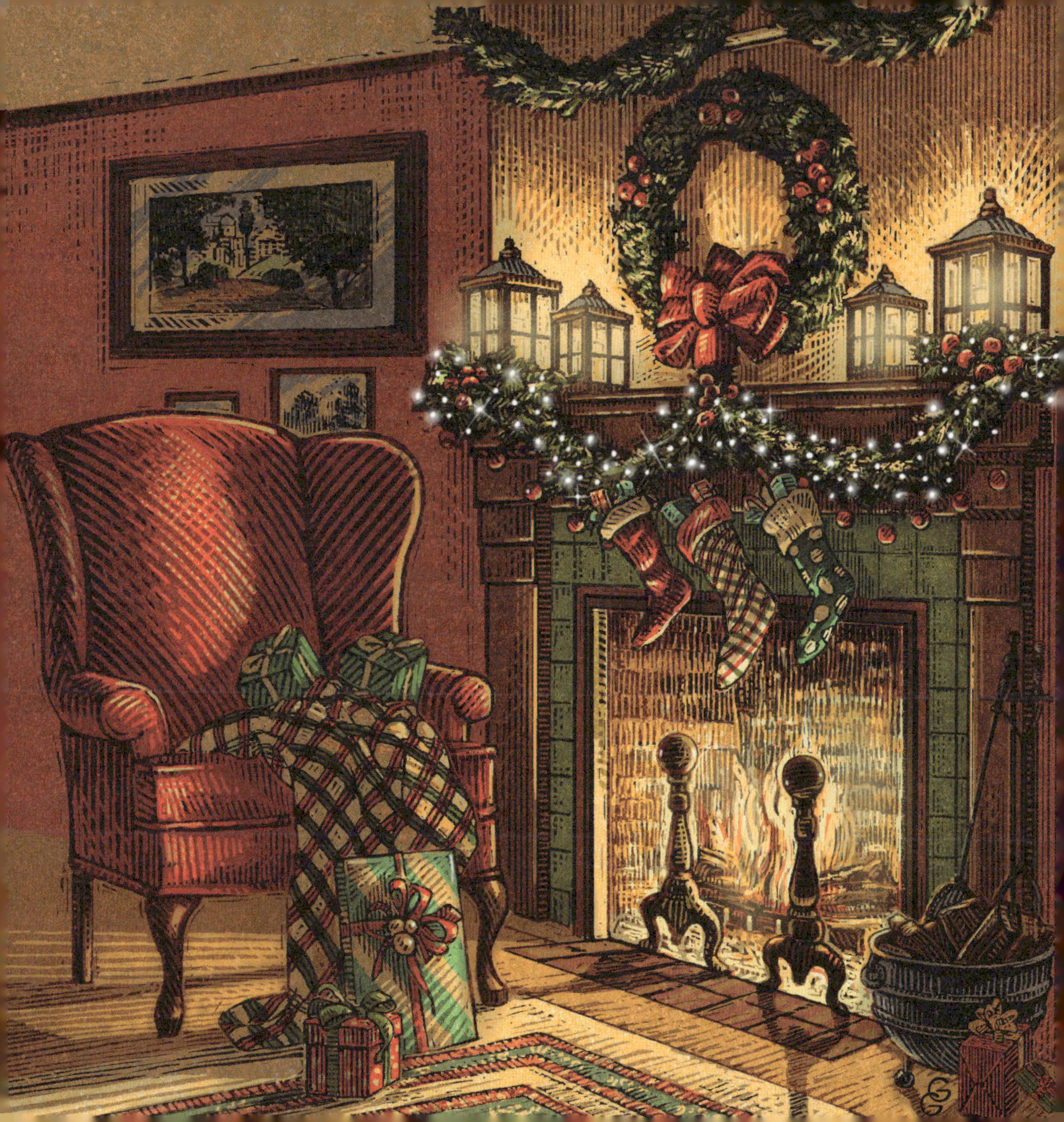

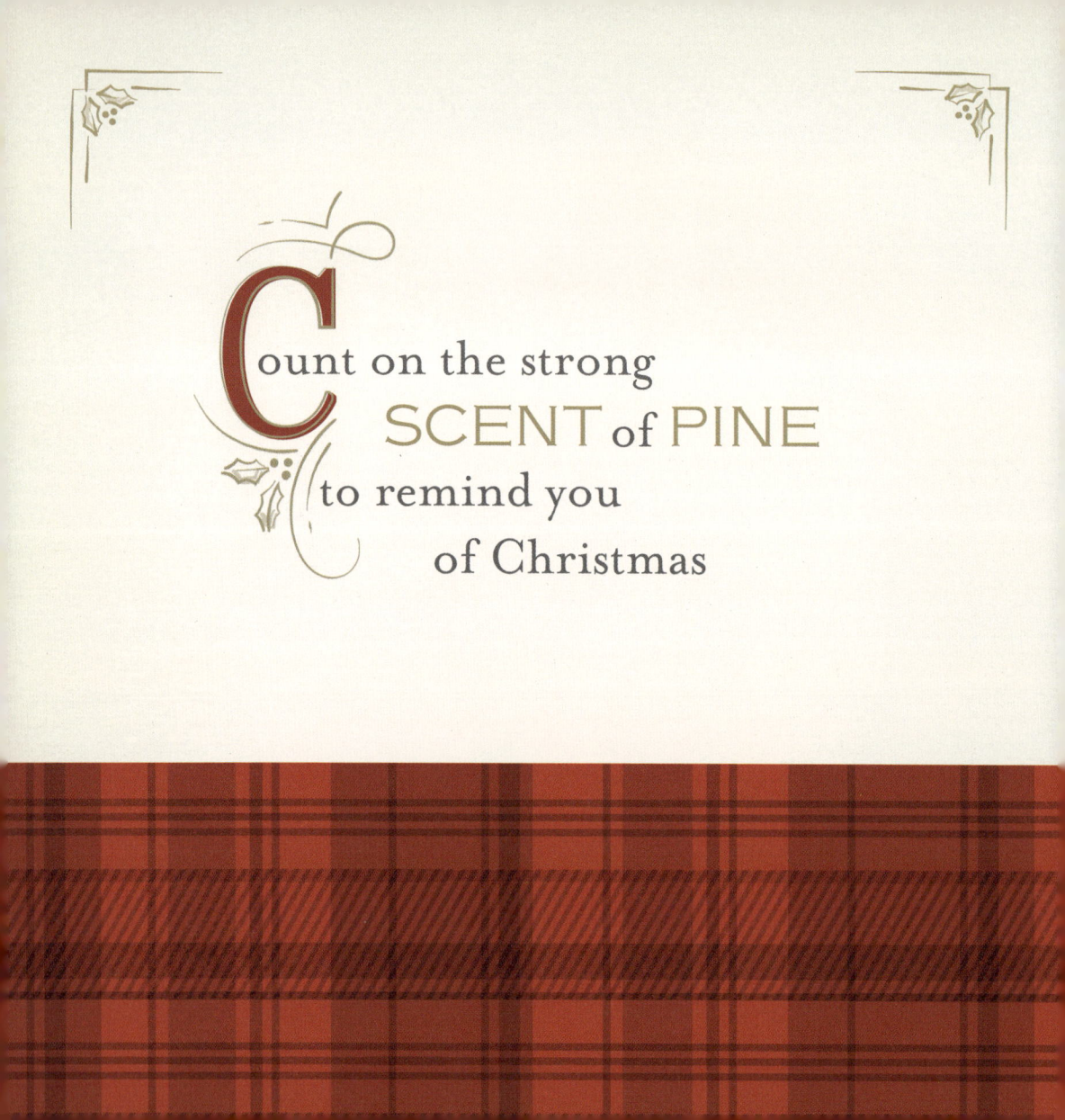

Count on the strong SCENT of PINE to remind you of Christmas

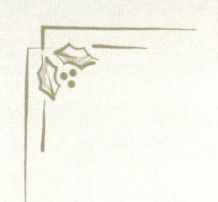

and a card
or a carol
to CONNECT YOU
with HOME.

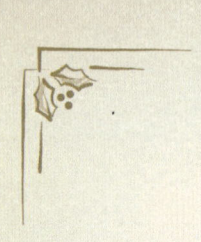

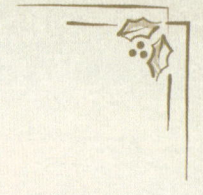

Count on strangers
to SMILE more
and wish your
LIFE MERRY.

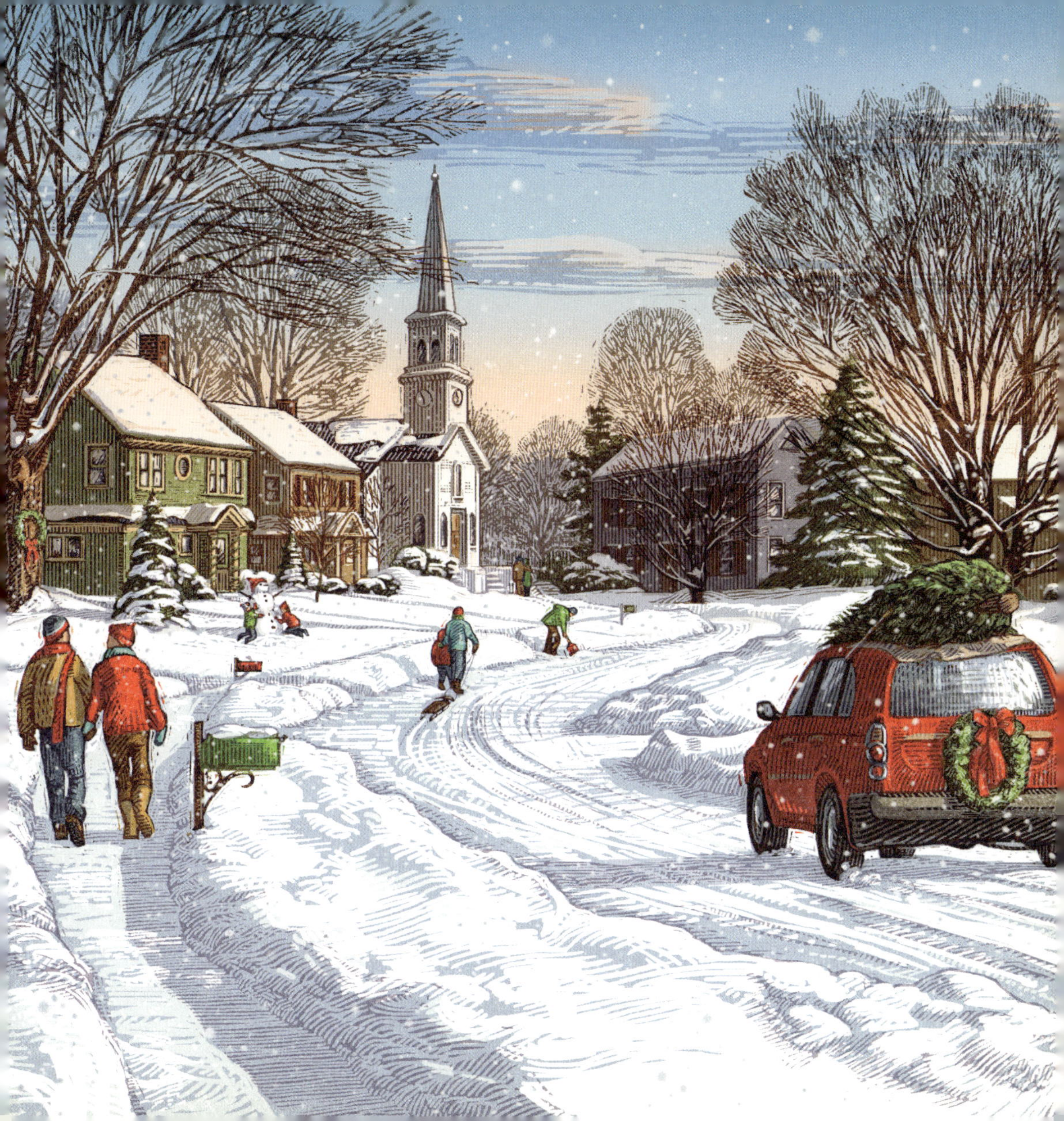

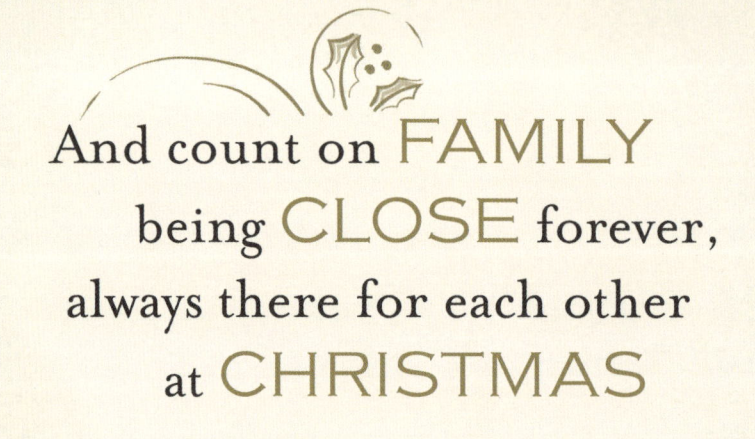

And count on FAMILY
being CLOSE forever,
always there for each other
at CHRISTMAS

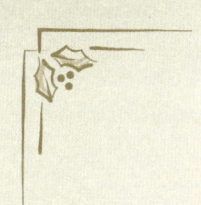

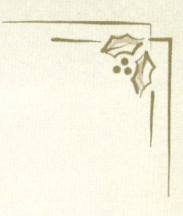

and all the other
MEMORABLE TIMES
that make a lasting impression
on OUR LIVES.

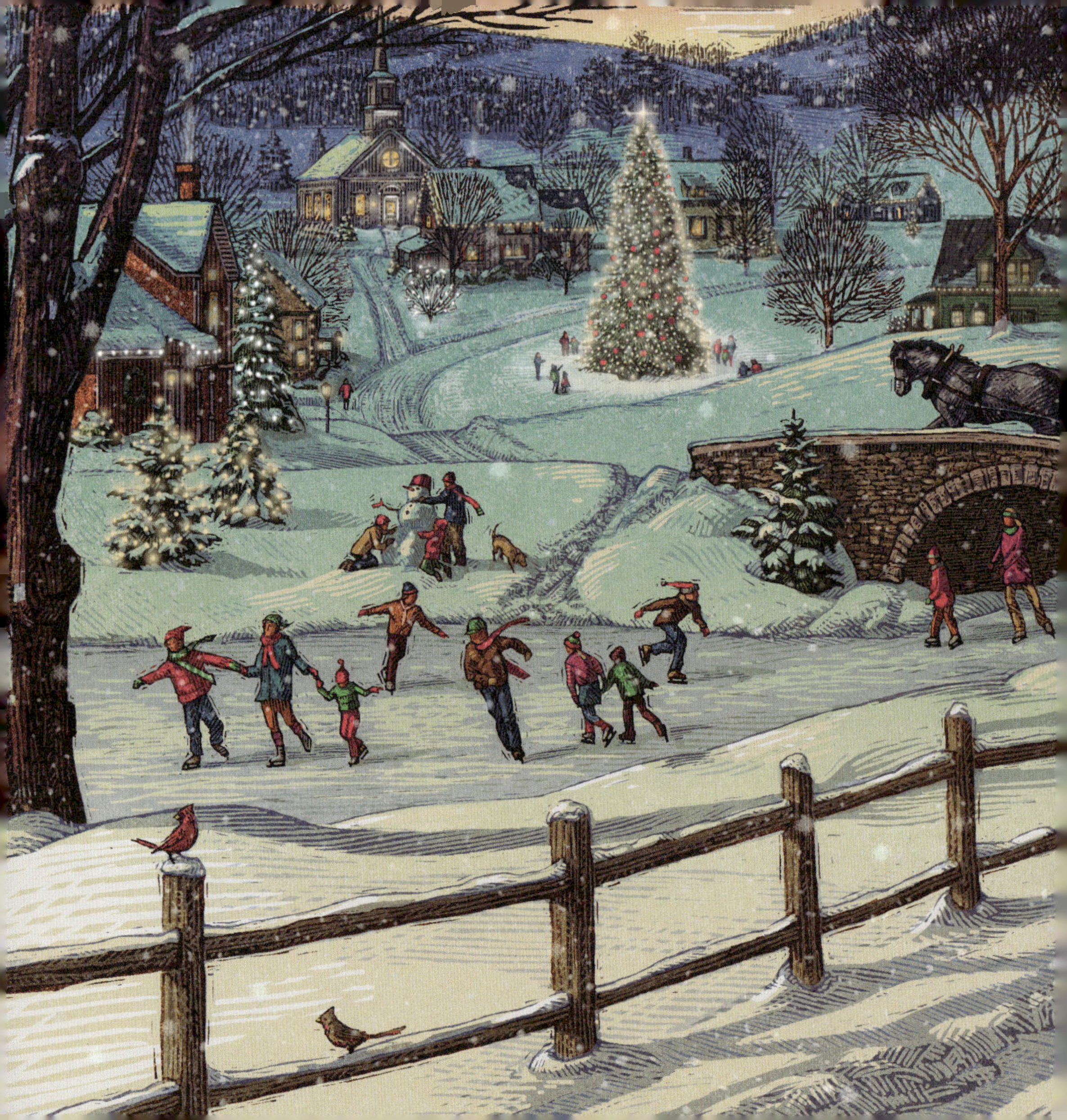

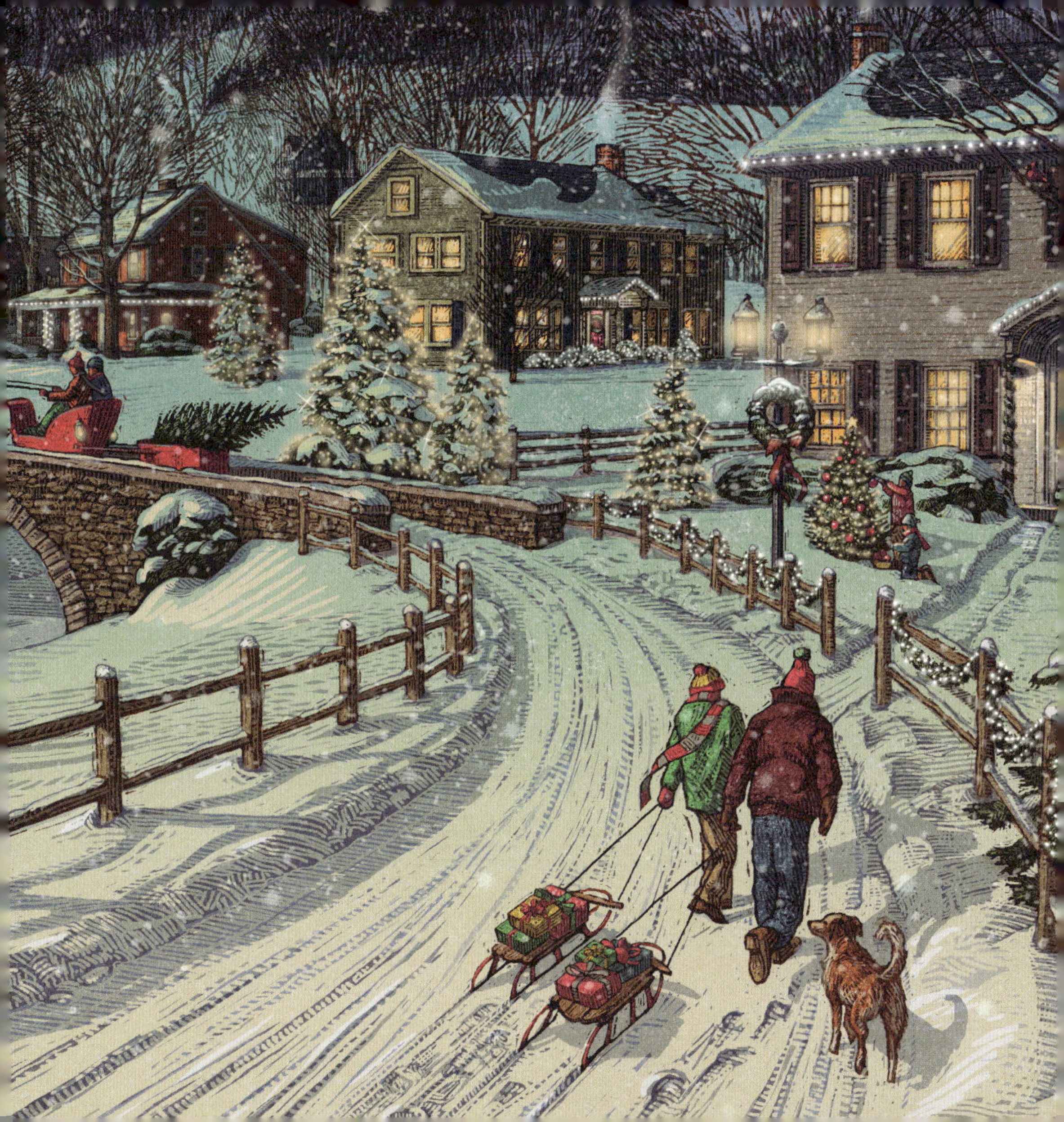

If every day were CHRISTMAS . . .

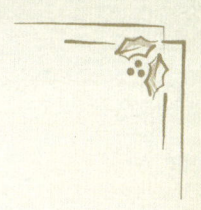

Everyone would take the time
to BE a little KINDER –

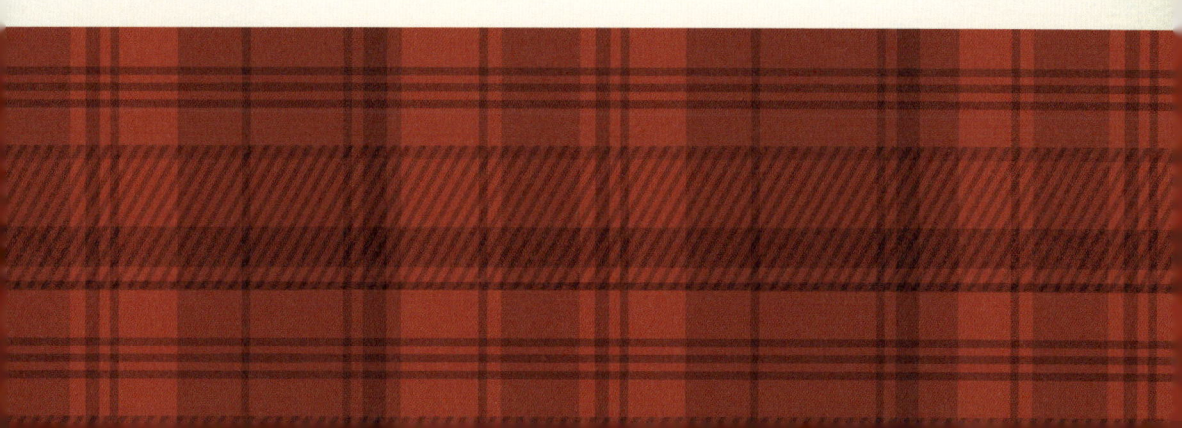

to be a little
MORE PATIENT
with one another.

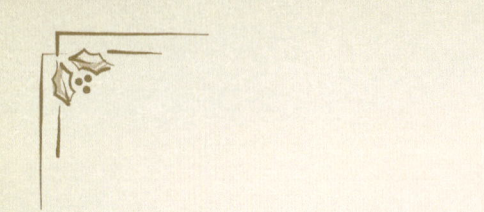

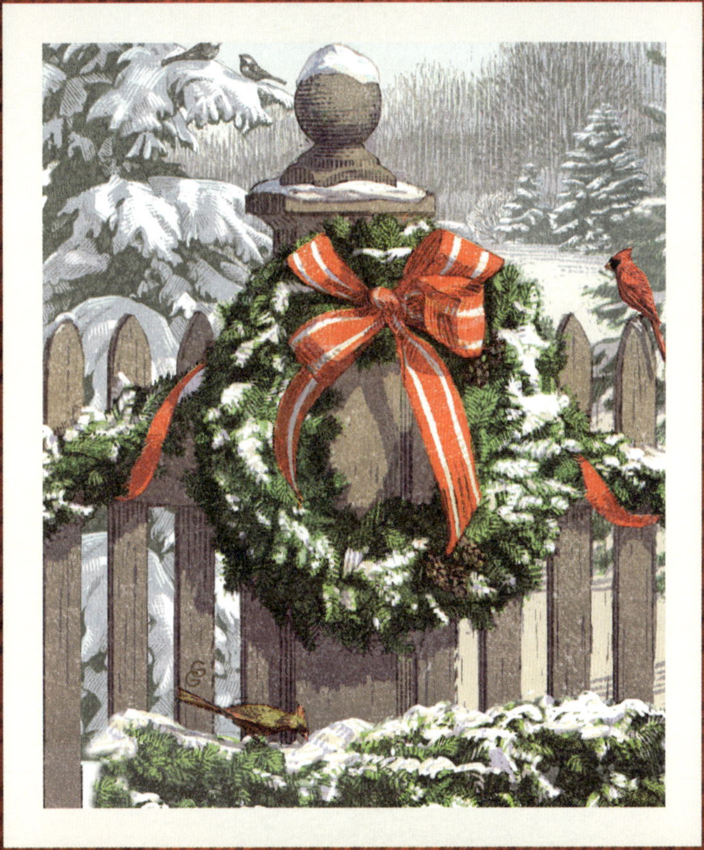

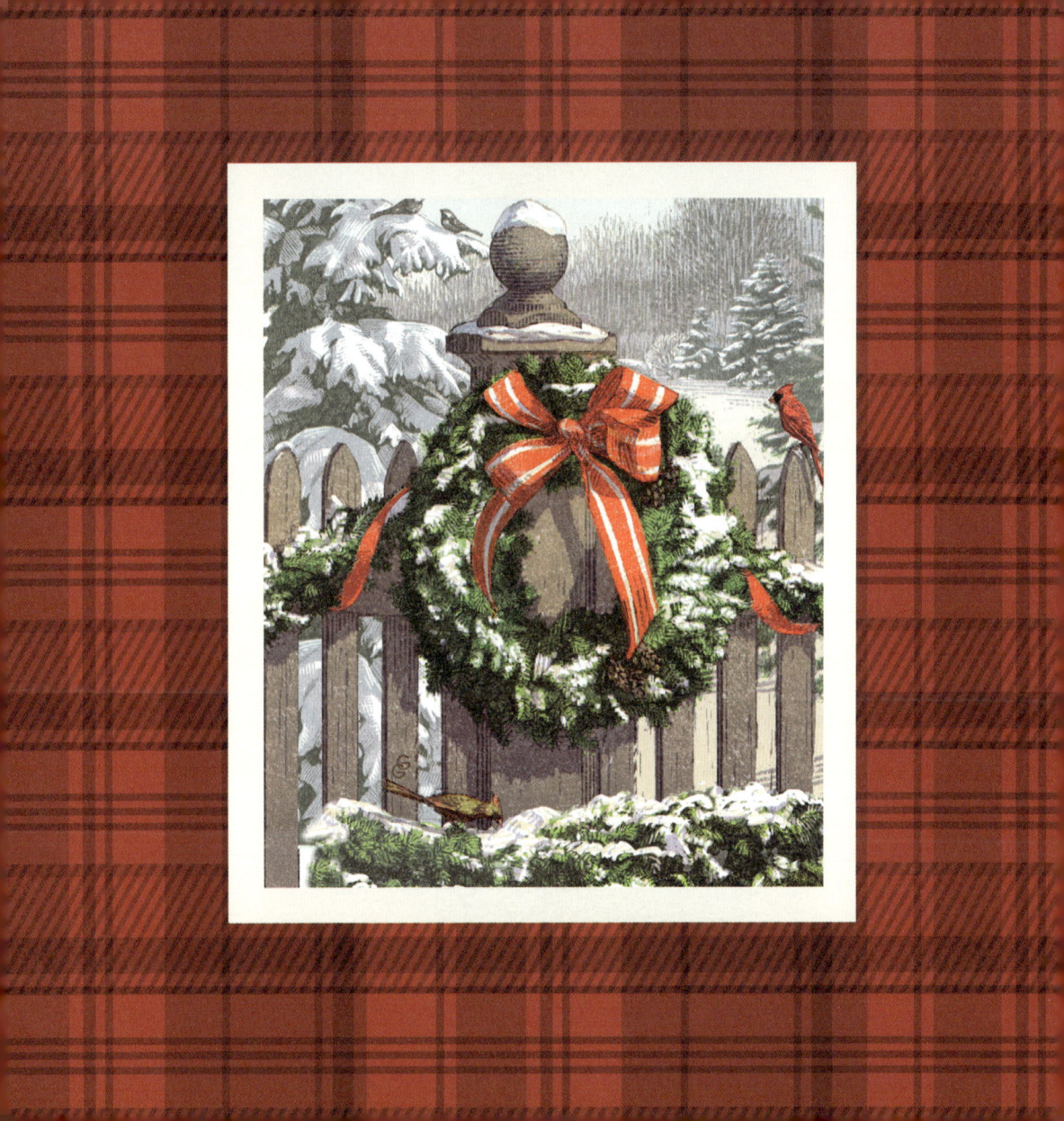

People would give
from their HEARTS

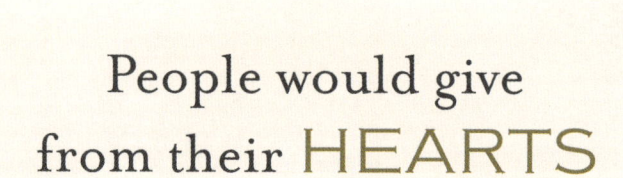

and lend each other a
HELPING HAND.

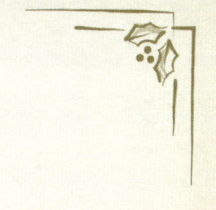

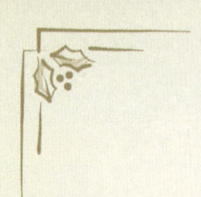

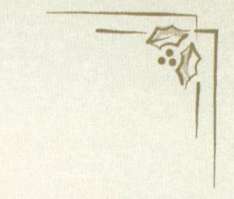

Friends would be
DEARER,
acquaintances would be
FRIENDLIER,

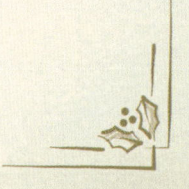

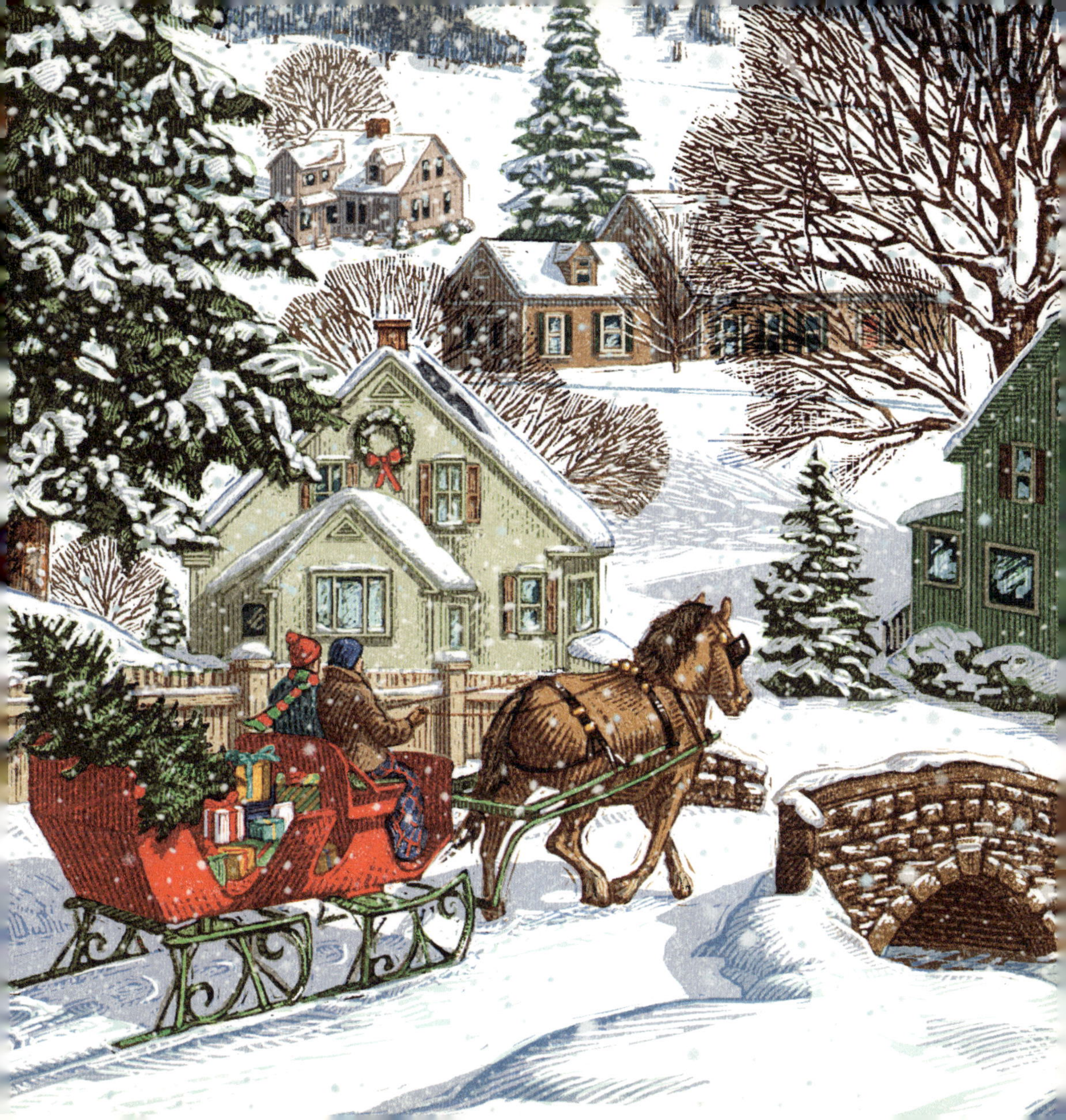

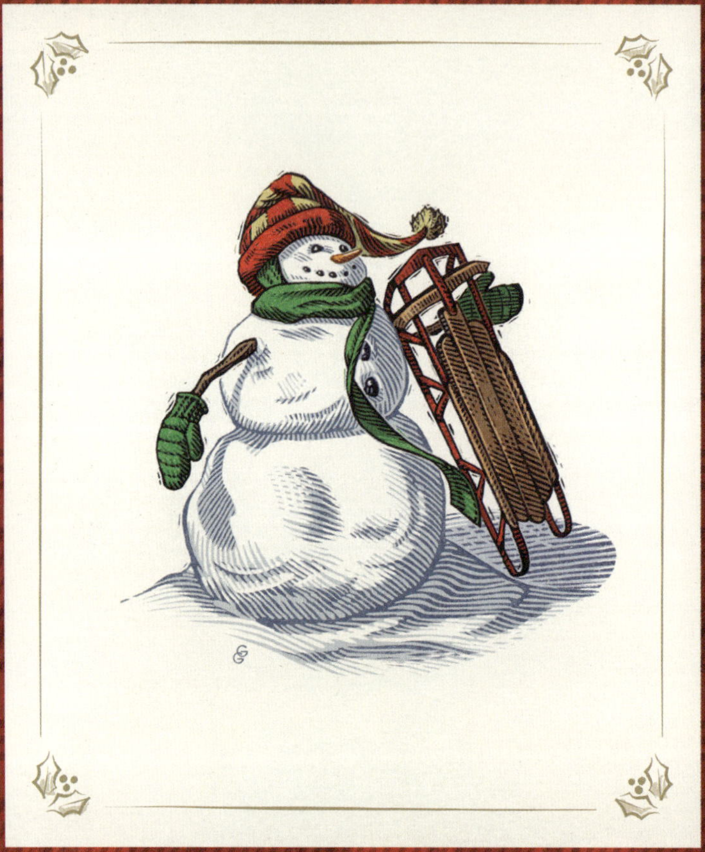

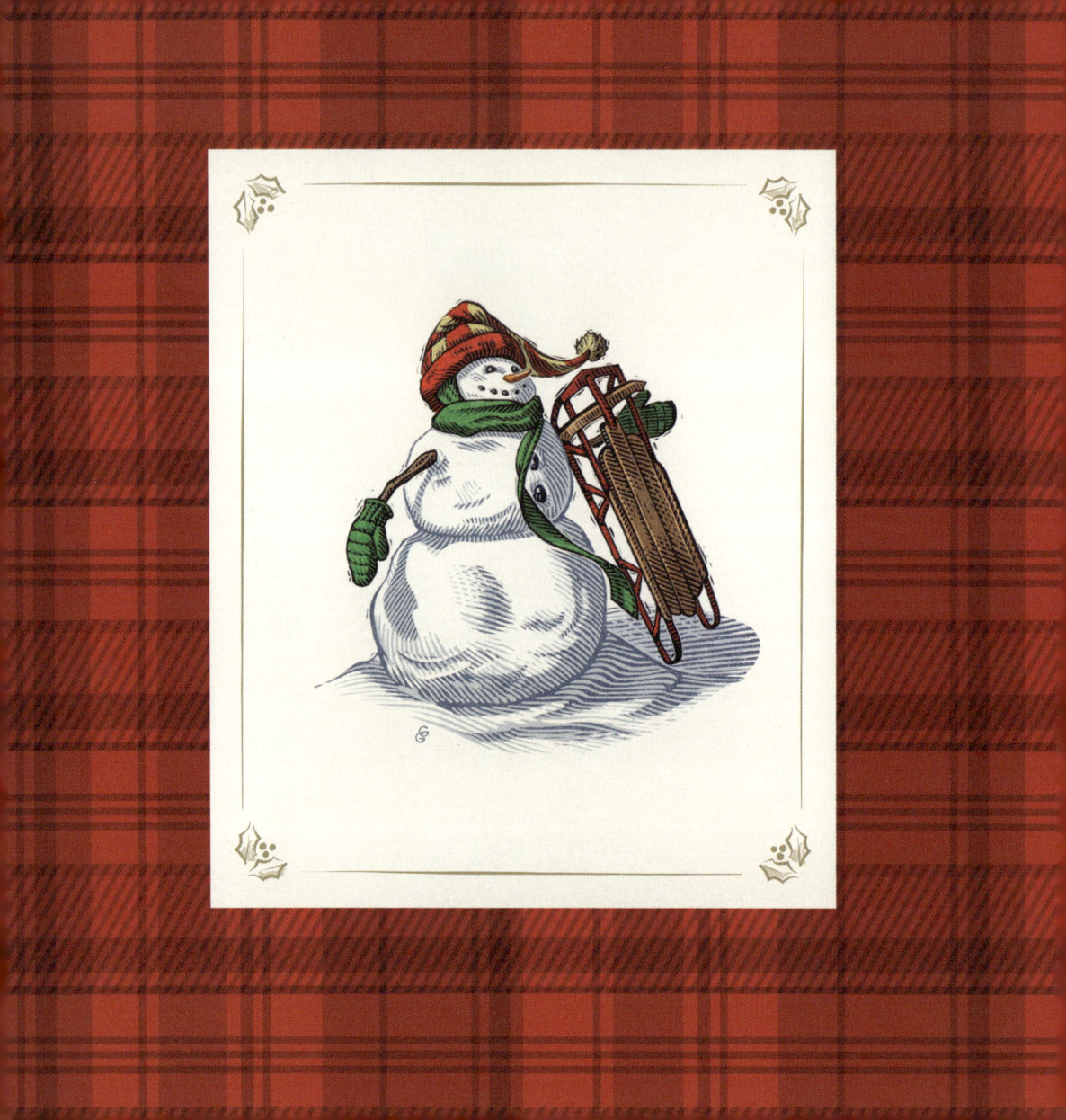

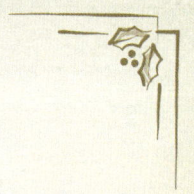

and complete
STRANGERS
would not hold back their
SMILES.

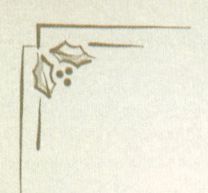

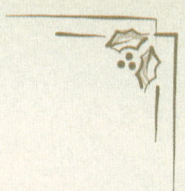

If every day were

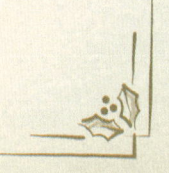

CHRISTMAS . . .

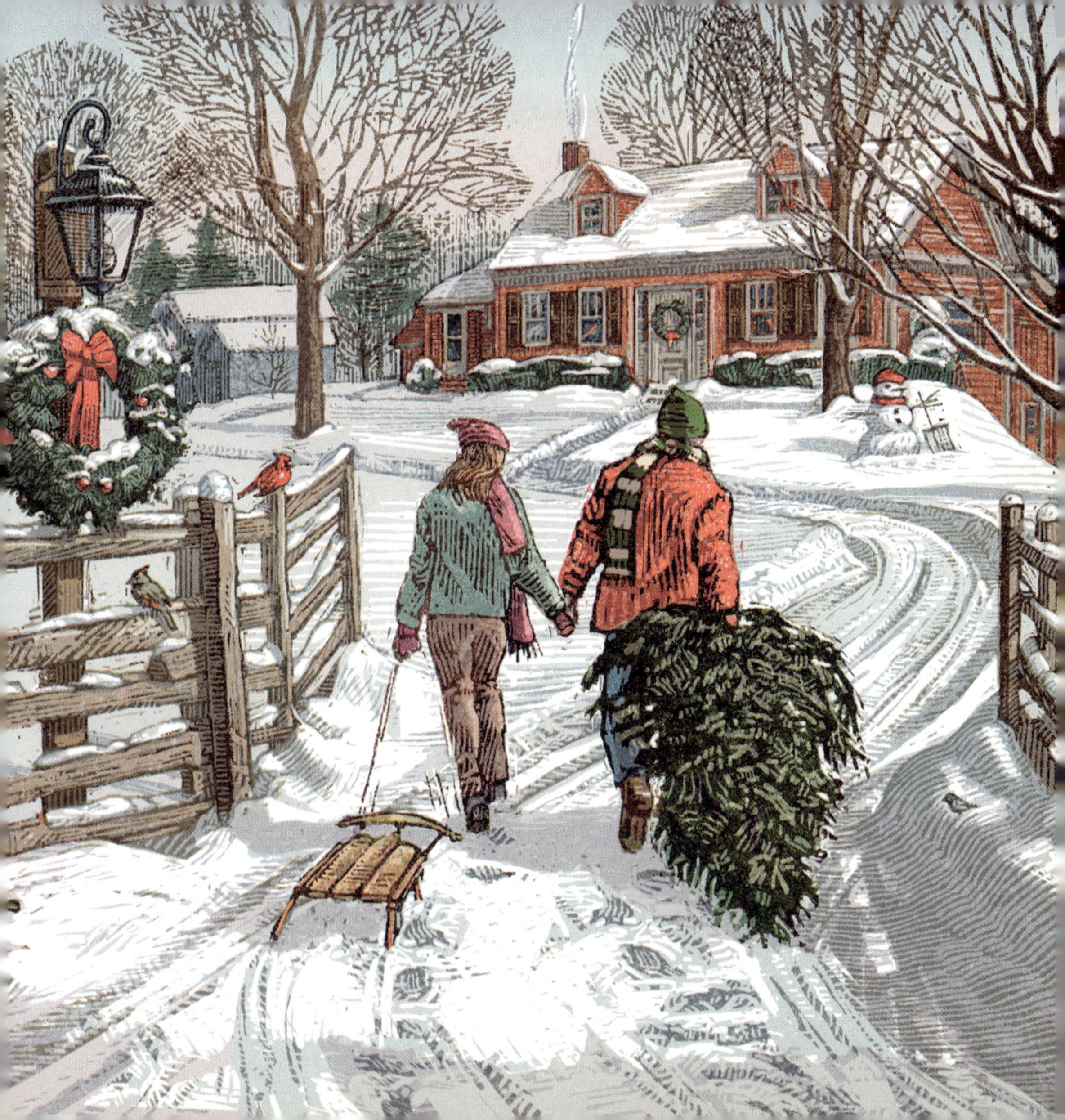

There would be more
HAND-HOLDING,
more HUGGING,

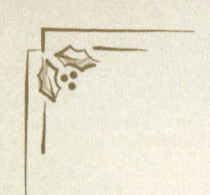

more HARMONY
in our voices,
and JOY would surround us
all like a blanket
of HOPE.

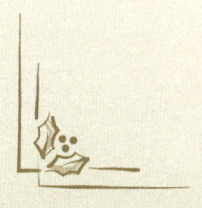

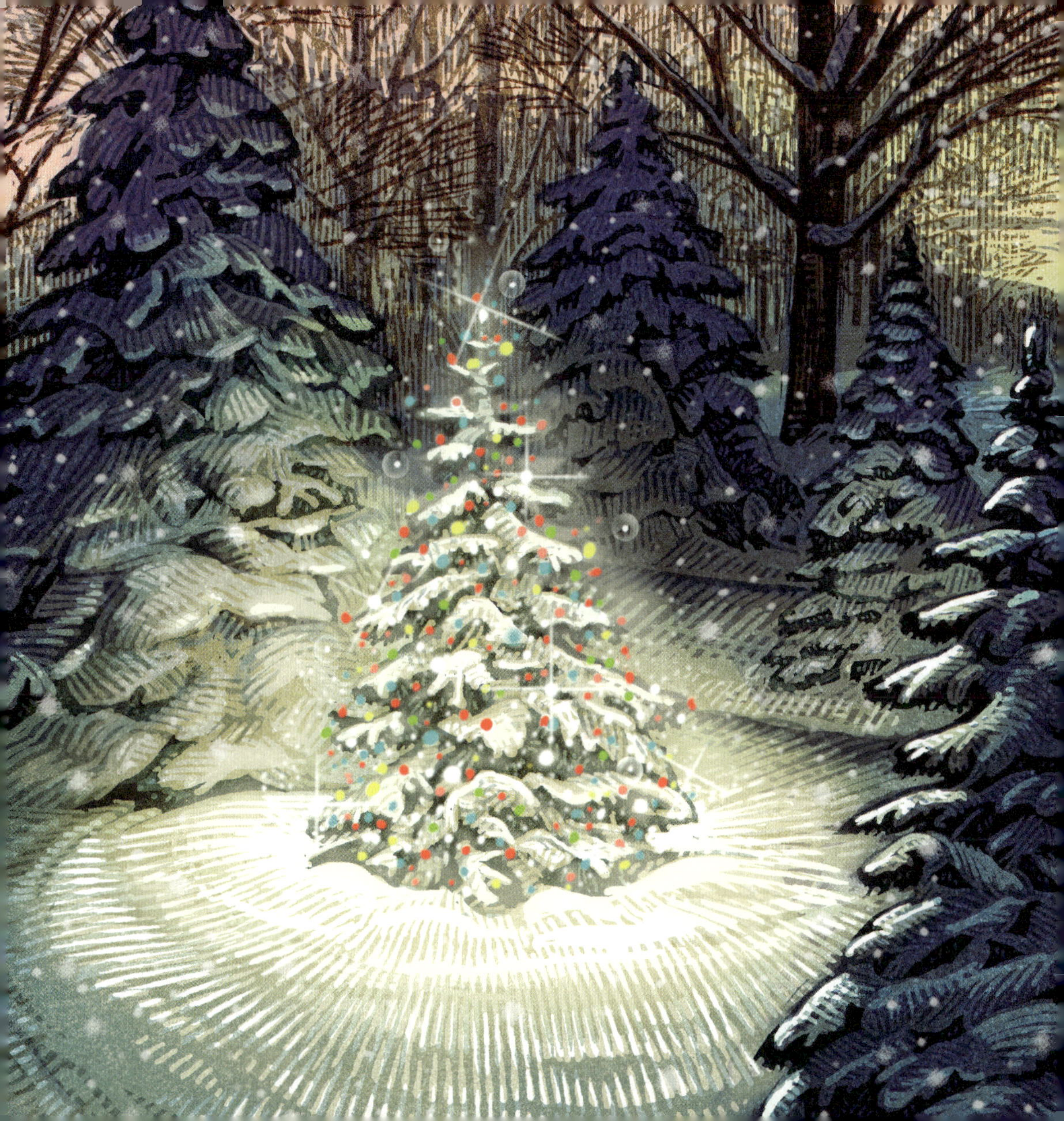

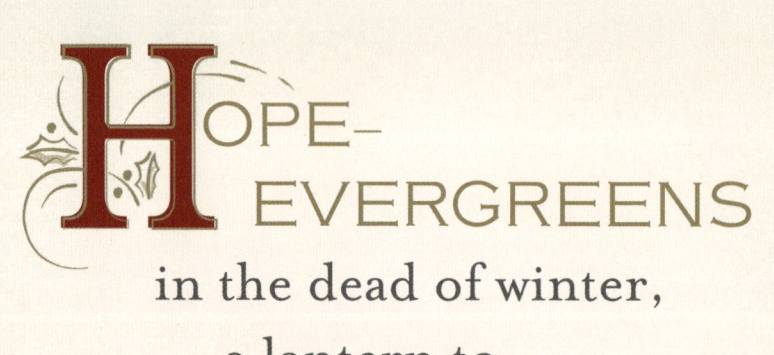

HOPE—
EVERGREENS
in the dead of winter,
a lantern to
LEAD the way home,
a bright star
to WISH on.

We never stop looking
for signs of HOPE,
but CHRISTMAS
reminds us it's always right here
in our HEARTS.

If you enjoyed this book
or it has touched your life in some way,
we'd love to hear from you.

Please write a review at Hallmark.com,
e-mail us at booknotes@hallmark.com,
or send your comments to:

Hallmark Book Feedback
P.O. Box 419034
Mail Drop 100
Kansas City, MO 64141

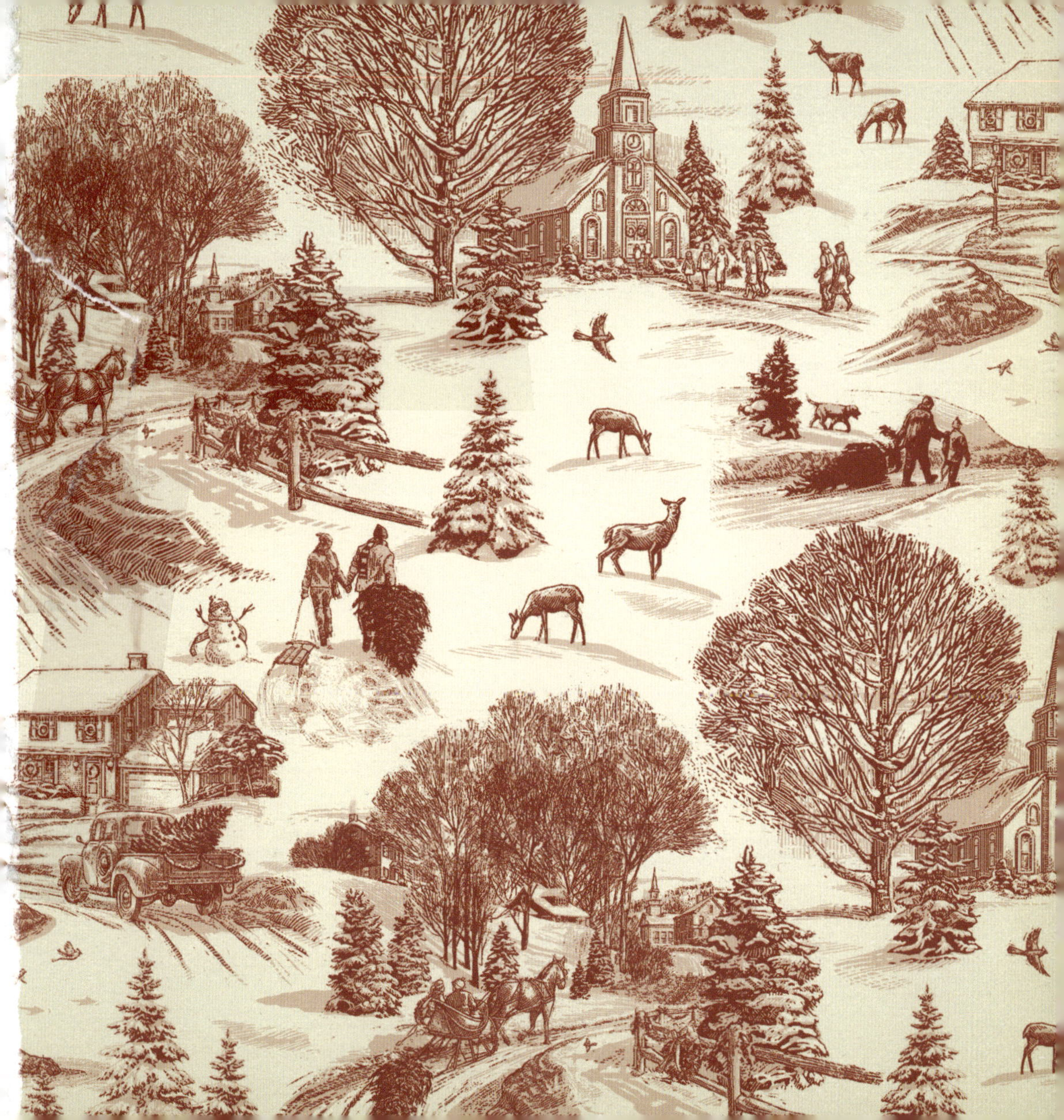